Stephen ———

(1152)

2015

The outside ___ me,

the inside ___ Him,

one flaw in the equation ___ me;

always charge to me.

This journey back home allows
us to focus on 3 things:

① Facing the future
② The privileges of the future
③ The purpose of the future

Go forth towards God knowing
that better is the end of a thing
than the beginning thereof.

Trouble doesn't last always!

Love
Canmer

In The Valley

Carmen Beck

WestBow
PRESS
A DIVISION OF THOMAS NELSON

WestBow Press books may be ordered through booksellers or by contacting:

WestBow Press
A Division of Thomas Nelson
1663 Liberty Drive
Bloomington, IN 47403
www.westbowpress.com
1-(866) 928-1240

ISBN: 978-1-4497-8840-7 (sc)
ISBN: 978-1-4497-8886-5 (hc)
ISBN: 978-1-4497-8841-4 (e)

Library of Congress Control Number: 2013905469

Scripture taken from the King James Version of the Bible.

Scripture quotations taken from the Holy Bible, New Living Translation, copyright 1996, 2004. Used by permission of Tyndale House Publishers, Inc., Wheaton, Illinois 60189. All rights reserved.

All Scripture quotations in this publications are from The Message. Copyright (c) by Eugene H. Peterson 1993, 1994, 1995, 1996, 2000, 2001, 2002. Used by permission of NavPress Publishing Group.

Printed in the United States of America.

WestBow Press rev. date: 3/21/2013

Oh that my words were now written! oh that they were printed in a book! That they were graven with an iron pen and lead in the rock for ever!

—Job 19:23-24

CONTENTS

ACKNOWLEDGMENTS

A word of thanks to my friends who know they hold a special status. To those who have laughed with me, cried with me, prayed and prayed and prayed with me. To those who have long been sounding boards for my poetry, dreams, and visions. To those who have nudged, scolded, and warned me into doing what God so lovingly called me to do. To those who have stayed supportive when I wanted to quit. To those still here. I am grateful.

Special appreciation also belongs to those who obediently allowed God to use them (whether they realized it or not) to bring the words in this book to life in me. Thank you for being the chisel in His hands; you helped change me.

And to Mika. Here's your coffee table book. I love you!

INTRODUCTION

Change. Isn't that what life and living are all about? When I talk about changes, I don't refer just to those we see when looking in the mirror and noting more wrinkles on our faces and bags under our eyes. I'm talking about the mental and spiritual changes that are only brought about through experiencing Jesus Christ. I often pray and ask the Lord to allow me to really see these important changes in me.

I invite you to come on this journey and experience the Lord with me. Come and see the changes that spending some twenty-one years in the valley brought about in my life. Come and see that no one who comes in contact with the Lord will remain the same. After all, it is said that experience is the best teacher.

I hope you'll enjoy what you find!

CHAPTER 1

HOW DID I GET HERE?

Who am I? Why was I born? How did
I get here? Where am I going?

God was thinking about me long before I was thinking about Him. I was born by His purpose and for His purpose. This life, then, is not about me. It is all about what He did first. I exist by His appointment, and I know that one is called out of the world and out of the darkness not by one's own will but by His. He called me out, and then He placed me in the midst of the valley.

"Wait, Lord! Wait," I cried. "Here? This is where You want me to be? Why here, Lord?"

The answer was plain and simple. There I would come to know and realize that my life is not my own, but rather I had been ordained. That means that I had been placed, purposed, set forth, brought into being, and have been chosen for a specific work. Funny how life is, but oddly part of a motto that once governed my career actually sums up the concept of God's ordination in our lives: [It's] "the only reason you and I are here."[1]

> Ye have not chosen me, but I have chosen you, and ordained you, that ye should go and bring forth fruit, and *that* your fruit should remain... - John 15:16

There is a certain way God would have you live, and there is a certain way to arrive where God wants you. Initially, I wasn't where I was supposed to be—even though I had been there a long time. And how I lived while I was there is another story in itself.

God knows me. He knows what I am. He knows what I am supposed to be. He knows what I can withstand, and He knows where I belong. He knows the way that I should take. But I needed to know. Then would I begin to understand what Jeremiah 18:1-6 means: "The word which came to Jeremiah from the Lord, saying, Arise, and go down to the potter's house, and there I will cause thee to hear my words. Then I went down to the potter's house, and, behold, he wrought a work on the wheels. And the vessel that he made of clay was marred in the hand of the potter: so he made it again another vessel, as seemed good to the potter to make *it* ... cannot I do with you as this potter? saith the LORD. Behold, as the clay *is* in the potter's hand, so *are* ye in mine hand..."

Out of the midst of

Called out of the midst of,
called out.
Before then I slept.
Walking and talking,
I slept.
Weeping and creeping,
I slept.
Tears for this world aren't real.
Looking for things in this life, hmm ... big deal.
What's the point
if I sleep?
But now,
called out of the midst of,
I seek
a higher calling.
I make my way toward the light
in hope,
by grace—
maybe, I just—
I just—
I just—
just might—
since I'm called out of the midst of—
I might lead someone
from wrong to right.
I might awake that soul
that sleeps so deep
as I slept before I was called
out of the midst of.
And just in case you're wondering
what will happen to me after today ...
out of the midst of this place
called He

—this one to stand and say and see—
I saw a better way;
and in seeing,
to know I'll be okay.
I'm out of the midst of.

Thou shalt call, and I will answer thee: thou wilt
have a desire to the work of thine hands. - Job 14:15

Out of the darkness He called me. He inclined my ears to hear and my heart to answer. He brought me into being. He chose me. Only after He chose could I respond, could I choose, could I answer. Would I accept or reject His offer?

One day I found that while my mouth was not open, my heart was speaking my answer. *Yes, Lord. Yes to Your will. Yes to Your way. To any way You want to use me, Lord, my heart says yes. I'll do what You tell me to do. I'll say what You tell me to say. I'll go where You tell me to go!* In my soul echoed the lyrics of Sandra Crouch's song, "Completely Yes":

> Yes, Lord, Yes, Lord
> from the bottom of my heart
> to the depths of my soul.
> Yes, Lord, completely yes;
> My soul says yes…
> My soul says Yes—Yes—Yes,
> Yes, Lord.[2]

I knew He had chosen me, and I knew that He knew the way I should travel. I couldn't see that path, and I didn't need to because He always knows.

The Lord knew my faith, and He knew that it needed to be better established if I were to grow in Him. It needed to be proven. It needed to be multiplied. That meant it needed to be tried. I needed to discover the depth of my attachment to my relationship with God. I needed to know that who I am and what I am about was not in me but *were* and *are* discovered in Him.

At the end of the day, I get on my knees and put the matter to consideration. I weigh it out, and I think it through. God chose. He called. He is the reason I am here. He has seen me through every rough and bumpy spot, every nick, every bruise, every hurt feeling, every hard lesson, every heated moment, every reason to cry, and through every time I thought I had to quit. In everything I encountered, He was there. And I have come to the conclusion that nothing I faced was really that bad. Why? Because He chose to place me just where I was at just the right time. My job, then, was to surrender.

10 - Carmen Beck

What does it mean to surrender? It means

- to give up possession or power over; to yield to another on demand or compulsion;

- to give up claim to; to give over or yield, especially voluntarily, as in favor of another;[3]

- to present yourself to another completely;

- to place yourself under the conduct and control of another;

- to resolve to do what another requires you to do;

- to follow the will of another;

- to not only submit to, but to comply with as wax does to the seal, to do what God pleases; and

- to die to yourself to live for another.

How easy to wonder when in a valley, "How did I get here?" Sometimes we think that when we accept Christ as our personal Savior and say, "Yes, Lord," that we are automatically entitled to mountaintop living. We think, *Good-bye hard times, trouble, and the downs of this life.* But I've learned that the opposite is often true. In fact, we sometimes have to go down, down in the valley, before we can go to the mountaintop.

See, the valley strips us of *me,* of *my,* and of *I.* The valley teaches us how to depend on Him. But how low must one go into the valley? Is not just being there enough to accomplish what is needed? Not when you still hold back from God, and surely not when you still hold on to that which He has said, "Surrender."

So in asking the question, "Lord, when I am as low as I can go what more would You have me do?" Quite possibly His answer will sound something like this: "Lower yourself before Me completely. Relinquish and empty yourself of you for Me. Allow yourself to be tried, to be proven, to be made over again. Allow yourself to be used by Me." The old hymn well states what our response to such promptings should be:

All to Jesus I surrender,
humbly at His feet I bow …
worldly pleasures all forsaken
Take me, Jesus, take me now.[4]

The valley is the place where I die that I may live for Him.

The emphasis is on the word "I".
What "I" want always gets in
the way of what He wants for
us.

CHAPTER 2

CAN THESE BONES LIVE?

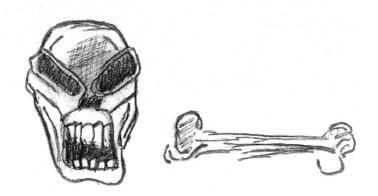

The hand of the LORD was upon me, and carried me out in the spirit of the LORD, and set me down in the midst of the valley which *was* full of bones, And caused me to pass by them round about: and, behold, *there were* very many in the open valley; and, lo, *they were* very dry. And he said unto me, Son of man, can these bones live? And I answered, O LORD GOD, thou knowest.

Ezekiel 37:1-3

The closer I get to God, the more I want to live and to see others come to the kind of life that is only found in Christ. Outside of Him it only seems one is living, but unfortunately, we find its death.

Dry like the desert;
one is dry.
No life.

I breathe;
I blow upon the soul.
Please, come to life.
No life.

I pray
for a light to shine
into this dark and dreary soul
that's cold—
very, very cold.

I whisper near to it,
"Please, come to life!
To live you must accept the life—
the light."

I pray.
Again, I say, I pray.

I blow
because the breath of life
I know is here.

Can these bones live?

The Bible teaches that each of us is born into sin; we are shaped in iniquity. As a result of the first couple's choice to sin, we are born into the society of death. We think, however, that we are living. But we do our "living" while swimming in a polluted stream. We are fooled into believing that we are truly living because our sin nature has so negatively affected our minds and has blinded our thoughts and understanding. In reality we merely exist.

Walking dead.
We are like bones.
We are the dry and walking dead.
No life.

I breathe;
I blow upon the soul.
Please, come to life!

No light,
no life,
no hope
without His breath.
Death.

Death in your eyes,
sunken and sullen.
Death in your walk,
worn and wavering.
Death in your speaking,
lifeless and lying.
Death in your actions,
desperate and dying.

Death in your cold, cold soul.

"The world, it offers a glimmer of light," you say.
That light is false
and fainting, fainting, fainting.

To really live requires that we be

- made alive,
- revived,
- nourished,
- preserved,
- repaired,
- recovered,
- quickened,
- restored, and
- regenerated.

Stephen — reading these words reminded me of the name of your group. Coincidence? I think not.

This gift of real living is freely given to all who accept Christ as Savior. Each person must make a choice to receive or neglect it. The life that is in Him overflows with the riches of His grace, His glory, and His mercy. Yet, sadly, not all want to live, to be revived, to be repaired, to be restored, and to be saved. Not all want to come out of the valley of the shadow of death. Imagine passively witnessing the acceptance of death!

The more I live, the more I want to see others live.

It is impossible for us to concoct real life. We can't call for a revival, a restoration, or receive salvation within ourselves by mere self-effort. After all, how can the dead raise themselves? We cannot breathe life or speak it into ourselves. We cannot call ourselves to get up and walk when we are dead. We cannot call ourselves from the grave. We cannot. But God can.

> Can these bones live?
> For a beating heart I listened
> on a cold and dreary day.
> At the setting of the sun, I heard the answer.
> God said, "I have the last and final say."

> "Thus saith the LORD GOD unto these bones; Behold, I will cause breath to enter into you, and ye shall live: … And ye shall know that I *am* the LORD, when I have opened your graves, O my people, and brought you up out of your graves, And shall put my spirit in you, and ye shall live, and I shall place you in your own land: then shall ye know that I the LORD have spoken *it*, and performed *it*, saith the LORD." – Ezekiel 37: 5-14

What is so appealing about choosing to live in a valley of death and dry bones? What makes us choose death when life is offered? What makes us want to remain in that state when grace is so freely given? Why not choose life?

In the valley I am dead, speechless, and silent before a Holy God; but when I accept Him I receive the outpouring of His Spirit and life!

Therefore, I shall not die but live and declare the works of the Lord. And the more I live, the more I want to see others live.

Just how bad is the situation? How cold is the body? How dry is the bone? I look in the mirror and I recall the state I was in; and I imagine someone thought, *Lord, she is beyond repair, beyond help, beyond saving.* And if it were not for the grace of Jesus Christ they might well be right.

Reflecting back, I stand thankful for how He changed me. No one is beyond salvation. There is hope in salvation for others as my heart is filled with the words of this song:

> "I heard a joyful sound,
>
> Jesus saves,
>
> Jesus saves." [5]

He saves all who will come to Him. The message of salvation and the hope of salvation are for all people. He is not willing that any should perish (stay dead), but He wants all to come to repentance (to be saved that they might live). Can bones live? I say they can.

> "To the utmost Jesus saves...
> He will pick you up and turn you around,
> Hallelujah, hallelujah Jesus saves." [6]

CHAPTER 3

STONES IN THE VALLEY

"Is my living in vain
Is my giving in vain
Is my praying in vain
Is my fasting in vain
Am I wasting my time
… Is my speaking, is it in vain?"[7]

Some days just aren't as good as others. Every now and then we all get down in the dumps; we all go through hard times, and sometimes we find ourselves needing someone to help pull us through them. Every now and then we all end up in valleys, wallowing in self-pity, sinking in shame, wrestling with unbelief, drowning in sorrow. And when that happens, we all need someone to come and see about us. Yes, every now and then we all need someone to pick us up and dust us off. We all need a smile, a hug, and the comforting assurance that everything is going to be all right. Every now and then we all need someone to meet us in our time of need. Every now and then we all need a friend.

> Why are you a part of my life,
> my friend, my friend?
> I call you my friend.
> You are my help to make my day a little brighter,
> to ease the burden and carry the load.
> You make them both a little lighter.
>
> To hold, to talk, and to walk.
> To speak and reach.
> To catch my hand.
> To pull me up and out.
>
> Oh!
> And then we both can shout
> and dance and sing
> because we made it out together,
> my friend, my friend, my friend.

We are our brother's keeper. We cannot have an attitude of *it's just about me*. The problems of this world are not overcome by one standing alone. God knew this and provided help for us in our time of need. Isaiah 61:1-3 says, "The Spirit of the LORD GOD *is* upon me; because the LORD hath appointed me to preach good tidings unto the meek; he hath sent me to bind up the brokenhearted, to proclaim liberty to the captives, and the opening of the prison to *them that are* bound; To proclaim the acceptable year of the LORD, and the day of vengeance of our God; to comfort all that mourn; To appoint unto them that mourn in Zion, to give unto them beauty for ashes, the oil of joy for mourning, the garment of praise for the spirit of heaviness; that they might be called trees of righteousness, the planting of the LORD, that he might be glorified."

The standard has been set, the example has been given. In the face of adversity, in the midst of the storm, in the heat of the moment, in the coldness of winter, in the darkness of midnight, in the face of all that seems so difficult, who will come to see about me? Who will stand and face the blistering wind with me? Who will fight the lion and slay the dragon with me? Who will climb the highest mountain or descend into the deepest depths of the valley to reach me? Who will stay with me in my time of need, in my time of despair, in my time of uncertainty, in my time of trouble? Who will continue to watch with me, will continue to fight for me, and will continue to pray for me? Who can I trust to pray? Who will have my back when the going gets tough? I need someone to stand on the same side as me within the struggle. I wonder who will be my friend.

> Why are you a part of my life?
> What is the reason that you come
> to heal and feel the pain,
> to laugh or cry,
> to share the beating drops, the coolness of the rain?
>
> To stay a while, provide the mothering comfort
> as though I were your child?
> To shape or sharpen
> as iron against the stone?
> To beat down with love
> and then to teach me how to get back up again—
> to help me rise above?
> To stand upon my feet—
> to stand and know—
> that piece by piece of who you are
> and you, and you, and you
> were used to make me
> who I am?
>
> Why are you a part of my life?

(I dedicate this chapter to my friend, Sandra Williams. May she rest in peace because as she lived a life as not unto herself, but always to others because she knew "it was not about her." July 3, 1958—February 10, 2008)

CHAPTER 4

WATCH AND PRAY

Watch out! Don't let your hearts be dulled by carousing and drunkenness, and by the worries of this life. Don't let that day catch you unaware, like a trap. For that day will come upon everyone living on the earth. Keep alert at all times. And pray that you might be strong enough to escape these coming horrors and stand before the Son of Man. - Luke 21:34 –36 (NLT)

Watching means

- to be on the alert, to be on the lookout;
- to look or observe, especially attentively.[8]

This place is dark,
and every day I'm forced to stay.
I must look up and pray to stay.

This is not my home;
thus, I watch and pray.

My eyes, they look.
My feet, they walk.
My soul must tarry here for now.
No rest nor sleeping here.
It's wrong—
for this is not my home.

My eyes, they look.
My feet, they walk.
My soul must tarry here for now,
but this is not my home.

This place is dark,
and every day I'm forced to stay;
thus, I watch and pray.

This world that I was born into, this place in which I have been called to exist for now, this is not my home! So why would I act as if it were?

As a child, my sisters and I would go on fishing expeditions with my father. We learned that because we were not home we needed to pay close attention and watch for danger. We needed to watch for strangers, and we needed to watch for snakes. We needed to watch where we walked and to take care where we chose to sit down. We needed to watch for even the signs of danger, such as a skin that a snake had shed, holes or burrows dug by animals, or strangers who lingered around too long. We needed to watch because even if something were not a clear and present danger, one could pop up at any moment. We had to watch because we were not at home.

One of the most important things we had to do was to stay close, to stay within hearing distance of our father. We had to watch, and we had to trust what he was saying so that the things around us—whether seen or unseen—didn't come upon us and overtake us. We had to believe him when he said that just because everything looked all right, didn't mean that it was. After all, we were not home.

And take heed to yourselves ... Watch ye therefore, and pray always...
-Luke 21: 34–36

How do I talk to God when I'm wandering in a valley? How do I
commune with Him? How and when do I make my petition known,
whether on behalf of myself or others?

Listening ears,
looking eyes,
loving heart.

Asking for prayer, needing prayer
Waiting, waiting, wanting prayer.

But will I pray?
Is it okay?
Tell me, Lord,
What will I say?

Whether in regard to the greatest thing or the smallest thing, the brightest day or the darkest hour, the mountain peak or the valley low, God is calling us to draw near to Him, to seek Him while He can be found, to call upon His name. He wants us to pray.

In the morning

a whisper,

at noonday

a song,

in the evening and at midnight

just a moan,

just a moan.

In the morning

my Father,

at noonday

my Lord,

in the evening and at midnight

Savior, Savior,

I call You, my own;

Savior, Savior

I call You, my own;

Savior, Savior

I call You, my own.

Prayer involves the sincere change of all of our mental, emotional, and spiritual processes. It requires us to move away from what is regular, what is arranged, and what is planned. It allows us to move away from using proper nouns, verbs, words, and sentences. It doesn't require that we be at the right place at the right time around the right folks. Prayer time isn't limited to kneeling at the side of the bed. It isn't relegated to the time when we bless the food or want to demonstrate devotion at church. It shouldn't be about hollering and screaming. We don't need to worry whether we are praying the way he or she would. Our words shouldn't be politically correct or incorrect. Prayer is about communing with God. God is calling us to look for Him, to look to Him, to come nigh and pray—even if we call from the valley.

CHAPTER 5

RUMBLINGS ON THE INSIDE

There is a life beating inside, as if in a cocoon.

The hard shell is all you're allowed to see right now.

But inside awaits the beauty of it all.

It's Spiritual

Crying is heard in the middle of the night.
And from my sleep I awaken to find
the crying is but me.

And in my soul I grieve to know
the meaning of it all.
Oh, in my heart I grieve to know
the meaning of it all.

Lord, can You share with me Your thoughts?
Or tell me why within my soul I hear the pitter-patter of a
heart
that cries with every beat it takes?
And why, within my mind, the thoughts are clouded deeply
like a fog that hovers there
and chokes the things
I once could think upon
to bring me peace and,
oh, such sweet serenity?

Lord, why within my soul
is it like a ghost is chained?
Through the temple of my soul
it drags the chains
and moans a dreadful moan
as if without a home?

Lord, why,
within my soul, do I hear
the dripping, dripping, dripping of tears?
Every drop is like the
dripping, dripping, dripping
heard within a hollow cavern.
It echoes, dripping, dripping,
dripping drops that man can never stop.

Lord,
deep within my soul a child is calling,
crawling, calling,
"Mother, Mother, can you hear me?"
Calling, "Mother, Mother—
Father is the name I now must call."

Father, can you take me?
Can you pick me up
and hold me in Your arms?

Can You save the child?
Free the ghost, Oh Lord!
Dry up the tears.
Explain the meaning of it all.

Father,
Thou hast all the answers;
I have none.
Thou hast all the time;
mine is on hand, for sleep will come again
and with the sleep will come the mystery.
Thus will start the questions
for the meaning of it all.

"Wisdom begins in wonder."[9]
—Socrates

And the angel of the LORD appeared unto him in a flame of fire out of the midst of a bush: and he looked, and, behold, the bush burned with fire, and the bush *was* not consumed. And Moses said, I will now turn aside, and see this great sight, why the bush is not burnt. And when the LORD saw that he turned aside to see, God called unto him out of the midst of the bush, and said, Moses, Moses. And he said, Here *am* I. –Exodus 3:2-4

Rumblings on the inside,
Rearranging my very soul.
There and there—right there, right here.
I feel parts and pieces moved around
Without, within.
You've been.

I feel You moving through
calling me still,
calling me still,
calling me still.

"Shh," I hear You whisper,
calling me still,
calling me still,
calling me still.

You are calling my name,
calling my name.
I hear You calling my name.

On the inside it comes to me,
piercing through my soul.
Your voice—it rolls, it rumbles, it walks, it talks.
It pulls me to You,
calling my name.
My mouth; it never answers.
Yet, my heart, it will:
"I hear You
calling my name,
calling my name,
calling my name."

Discernment is insight. It is a power and awareness to see what is not evident to the average mind. It is not based on the ordinary point of view, human knowledge, or the understanding of a carnal mind. But is the quality of being able to grasp and comprehend what is obscure.

When God shows you what He shows you, when He tells you what He tells you, do you believe? Do you dare *not* believe? Do you want to see things as He sees them, or do you want to see things as you see them? Do you want to know the truth? The reality of it all?

> Faces, scenes from some familiar place but yet,
> it's made to seem as though I dream with eyes awake.
> I see what is to be.
>
> You speak.
> I see pictures, visions clear and plain.
> And I hear You
> calling my name,
> calling my name,
> calling my name.

Unless you are able to discern what is of God and what is not, unless you can discern what is really going on in a situation and what is really important and why, then you will always make the wrong decisions. You will always second guess yourself, and you will always second guess God.

The problem most of us face is that we want everything to make logical sense. We've learned that one plus one plus one equals three. And to us that equation will always equal three. But does God always see it that way? And when He says that one plus one plus one does not equal three, will we believe Him? Will we see it the way He sees it? Can we find it in ourselves to accept His reasoning that with Him, when it's about Him, One is always the answer?

I spoke it.
Were you listening?

I showed it.
Did you see?

I touched you on the inside with My Spirit.
Did you feel?

Am I real?
Am I real?
Just how real?

When a man goes on his natural perspective (what he thinks and what he feels) and on his own self-chosen ways and whims instead of on the path of wisdom that is God's way, life can only end in death. The one walking and going forth in the understanding of God, however, will be led by the Spirit and will quickly remove himself from evil. That person will be eager to grow in understanding, to feed and nourish that understanding, and to live in it—even if it leads him to places he's never been or to places he would rather not go—even if it leads him to the valley. That person will come to understand that God's way and His path are the best way and the best path. That person will be ready to go with God anytime, anywhere, and through anything; and he or she will be prepared to go all the way.

Now do you believe in Me?
Look.
See.
Feel.
I'm real.

CHAPTER 6

I WILL FEAR NO ...

Yea, though I walk

through the valley of the shadow of death,

I will fear no evil:

for thou art with me...

-Psalm 23:4

What dark evil does this day bring?

Oh, if we could see all that is around us, all that the naked eye alone cannot see; if we could hear the thoughts in the minds of others, those voices in the spiritual realm that are both for us and against us; if we knew the intentions of others towards us; if we understood that there is an evil one seeking to devour us; if we would just remember, we would know this is not our home.

Eyes are upon me;
in darkness, they shine in the night.
Sounds are around me,
stirring and mocking my soul to faint
and put me to fright.

Above, around, beyond, in front is dark.
I walk.
The dark is near to snatch and catch me.
I do not run.
I walk.

Above, around the sound says, "Kill."
But still,
I walk.

The mountains high,
the valley low.
I go, I go, I walk.

It were that from beyond the dark
you pounce;
and every inch and every ounce
you would but take and break and kill.
You want to kill.
You would not stop just to hurt—but to kill.

Yet still, I walk.
And I will fear no evil.

To fear is to be greatly terrified, whether of things seen or unseen; whether of lions, or of tigers, or of bears. And when one is surrounded by the enemy, when nothing appears except that which is discouraging, when the number against us appears to be more than the number for us, when the situation looks extremely hopeless, when it appears the enemy has us boxed in, we may give way to fear.

Too big for me today.
Something is too big for me today.

Above my head,
beyond my reach,
outside the bounds for which I can go
and the goals that I can meet.
Something is too big for me today.

I looked up, and it was there—
as high as I could see.
I looked left, then right,
and it was there,
as far as my eyes could see.
I looked, and all that I could see was *it*.

Fear or trust in the living God?

Are you willing to face the storm? Willing to face the unknown? Willing to face the fears ahead despite the possibility of failure? Despite the possibility of grave and great danger or pain or trouble? Are you willing to face the valley of the shadow of death? Are you?

Matthew Henry said,

"The ruin of some of the enemies of God's people is an earnest of the complete conquest of them all. And therefore, these having fallen, he is fearless of the rest: Though they be numerous, a host of them, - though they be daring and their attempts threatening, - though they encamp against me, an army against one man, - though they rage war upon me, yet my heart shall not fear."[10]

Speak stillness to your fainting heart,
for God is near.

We tend to look at something or someone and attribute power. For instance, at hearing a certain word like "cancer" or because someone holds a certain position or title, we automatically make the situation or the person larger than life itself.

To all who have run into the giant of cancer, drinking, drugs, peer pressure, incurable disease, homelessness, or abuse, know that bowing to the thing gives it power; stand up to the thing, and honor is gained. Fear not; instead, know to whom and what to surrender.

> "Ride on King Jesus
> no man shall a-hinder me.
> Ride on King Jesus
> Ride on
> No man shall a-hinder me
> —no man shall a-hinder me."[11]

Fear not. Trust and have faith in the living God for there is no enemy and no thing that cannot be conquered by Him.

Quit!
Quit walking upon me
as though you have power over me.

God is above,
and He sees.
He knows.
And He with His hand
can stop.

Quit!

Quit
raising your voice,
flexing your plex,
making your threats
as to put fear in my soul …
as to put doubt and trembling in my walk.

Don't you know who is really in control?

God is above,
and His voice is one that causes
mountains to quake,
evergreens to bend,
waters to still,
men to live or die.

Quit!

CHAPTER 7

PEACE IN THE VALLEY

Like a snow globe that is shaken up with flurries
going round, disturbed above our heads,
life is moved out of order.

Life, once controlled and quiet
is turned topsy-turvy.
Life is a noise that can only be heard
within my head.

Life is tilting
and talking
and moving
and shaking
and turned upside down
and there's nowhere for you to go to be unmoved.

The grip you had
is slipping,
and slipping,
and slipping.

All you want is for all to stop
shaking and moving.

You want quiet
and still
and peace.

All you want
is for the snow to settle
and the sun to shine
and the noise to stop.

Quiet
and still
and peace
in the valley.

And he arose, and rebuked the wind, and said unto the sea, Peace, be still. And the wind ceased, and there was a great calm. - Mark 4:39

W hat exactly is peace? Peace is

- a condition of freedom from disturbance, whether inwardly or outwardly;

- a quality describing a society or a relationship that is operating harmoniously;

- wholeness for well-being;

- the absence of war or conflict;

- absence of strife, whether internally or externally;

- the restoration of order;

- reconciliation;

- tranquility within and without oneself.

What is the message of peace? It is for all movement to cease that we might be at rest. It brings tranquility to the soul and tranquility on the earth. It asks that all disturbances, no matter what they are, come to an end. It is the hope that wherever I am, wherever I find myself, there will be peace—even in the valley.

What is the message of peace? It summons order, attention, and reverence in His holy presence. It points to His power, authority, and majesty; and ushers in praise as it is well described and sang by the great voice of Rev. James Cleveland:

> "The wind and the waves shall obey My will. Peace, be still!
> Whether the wrath of the storm-tossed sea, or demons,
> or men, or whatever it be, …
> Peace, be still! Peace, be still!
> Oh—Peace …"[12]

What is the message of peace? It calls for the havoc of this world wrought by the hands of man to come to an end. It applies to those with skin that is black, red, or white; to the Jew and to the Gentile; to the rich and the poor. It speaks of a time when the wolf and the lamb will rest together without fear. It points toward the reconciliation between man and earth, between man and creature, between man and man, and between man and God.

"Peace, be still! Peace, be still!
Oh–Peace." [13]

What is the message of peace? Peace means no more sickness in the body, no more tears, no more death, no more sorrow, no more worrying about what will come tomorrow. It means no more headache, heartache, and pain. With it come no more violent disturbances in the body or in the soul. It is rest.

" ...Torrents of sin and of anguish
sweep over my sinking soul!
And I perish! I perish, dear Master;
O hasten, and take control ...[14]

What is the message of peace? It means no more stormy days. It looks forward to a day and a time when all the earth will stand silent before Him. It is the hush that signifies our surrender in humble submission and obedience to His will.

"Peace, be still! Peace, be still!
Oh–Peace ..."[15]

What is the message of peace? I believe it is a message of expectation. You can know that wherever you are, there can be and one day there will be peace! There is a river, the streams of which will make glad the city of God, and peace will come to those who belong to Him.

God gives us peace when we are in Him. When we don't feel peace, then, we must wonder whether we have walked away from it. Have we stopped searching for it, listening for it, and walking in it? "Peace I leave with you," Jesus said in John 14:27, "my peace I give unto you: not as the world giveth, give I unto you."

What is the message of peace? It is knowing that in the end—even when it seems we can't find our way out of the valley—there will be peace.

Whispering Peace

Hovering above the plain
there is peace.
To the edge of the end
I have to go,
so I will know it is there—and there it should be everywhere.

Calming and captivating,
peace is ever waiting to be plucked
out of the air.

CHAPTER 8

IN TIMES LIKE THESE

We are troubled on every side, yet not distressed; *we are* perplexed, but not in despair; Persecuted, but not forsaken; cast down, but not destroyed ... For which cause we faint not... - 2 Corinthians 4:8-18

But not ———
Words of strength.

But not ———
because God has not
given up.

E ndurance is
  • staying;

  • stamina;

  • perseverance;

  • holding out;

  • holding on;

  • persisting in determination;

  • continual pursuing that usually takes place over a long period of time—especially despite difficulties.

Over one hundred years is a long time to exist in a situation; wouldn't you agree?

Day after day, after day, after day existing in the same situation.

People coming, people going.
Babies being born.
Old friends, family, children, dying.
And you?
Existing.

We have a tendency to give up quickly, but God calls us to persist. In prayer; persist in believing, and persist in holding on. Persist in asking; keep on seeking, keep on knocking, keep on keeping on. Stay; stand, and be that much more determined to endure until the end.

Year after year, day after day,
time after time again—
existing.

Over one hundred years is a long time to exist in a situation; wouldn't you agree?

Not much, sometimes to say.
Not much, sometimes to do.
Not much, nothing sometimes—
but wait.
Exist.

God wants you to endure, to persevere, to stay, to determine to prevail through trials, battles, and the valley. You must remain determined. That's how God wants you. You may stumble a little bit, getting tired and weary; but God wants you to stay determined. He wants people who will travail to prevail. God wants people who will hold out and hold on, enduring until their change comes. God wants those who are determined to wait on Him until the end—even when they find themselves in a valley.

"In times like these
You need a Savior.
In times like these
You need an anchor.
Be very sure, be very sure
Your anchor holds
And grips the Solid Rock!"[16]

Endure! Hold on firmly until the end. Have undying continuance. Press forward and beyond your normal limits. Do not draw backward, but hold your ground. *Reach, grasp above and beyond the situation.*

How long?
How much and when?
Just when I think it's over,
I'm back where I begin.

Over one hundred years is a long time to exist in a situation;
wouldn't you agree?
My soul longs to leave here.

My heart hurts for home.
My mind thinks on what's not here
and wonders whether I'm all alone.

Over one hundred years is a long time to exist in a situation;
wouldn't you agree?

Constancy means

- to stand the state or quality of being unchanging;

- to have firmness of mind or purpose, resoluteness;[17]

- to be stable and not wavering.

We all want relief. We want our problems, our sicknesses, our trials, our headaches, and our body aches to hurry up and go away. We want whatever is causing us grief, worry, or pain to just leave. We want the storms and the clouds of life's valleys to just hurry up and go away!

And yet, the relief and rest we want sometimes come only when we accept the fact that all of our suffering, our trials, our headaches, and the frustrations of our valleys are things we are destined to endure. See, there are some things we must face in this life. We must accept this and then gather strength to endure and overcome.

Bones get frail,
limbs get weak,
voices get quiet,
eyes get dim,
heartbeats get slower
and slower
and slower.
Existing.

Over one hundred years is a long time to exist in a situation;
wouldn't you agree?

That is why we never give up. Though our bodies are dying, our spirits are being renewed every day. For our present troubles are small and won't last very long ... So we don't look at the troubles we can see now; rather, we fix our gaze on the things that cannot be seen. For the things we see now will soon be gone, but the things we cannot see will last forever. 2 Corinthians 4:16–18 (NLT)

Did someone forget I was here;
forget to call my name?

What does it matter?
Every day is like the next day,
and the next day,
and the next day.
They are all the same.

If I cry,
does anybody hear me?
Does anybody comfort me?
Does anybody care?
I stop; I ask,
"Why? When will all of this be done?"

Over one hundred years is a long time to exist in a situation;
wouldn't you agree?

Why do we face these experiences, these times, these afflictions, these trials and tribulations, these storms, and these valleys? What purpose do they serve? Exactly who is benefiting from them?

Sometimes we are brought to extremes and have to go through them, but we dare not trust in ourselves. We must remember while enduring despair and valleys that we should not hope in ourselves and not think our help will come from within us. Sometimes it's only when we go above our strength and our ordinary, normal limits that we recognize that He is our strength! Sometimes it's only when we are wearing out and are worn out and find ourselves decaying slowly that we come to realize that this is not our home. Further, to move closer over there we must start pulling up roots over here. Why? So that all this can pass away, so that all that He has for us can be added. Enduring helps us to be sure, very sure.

We put a limit on how long we want to go through something. We say we've had enough, and we give it a date and a time as to when we will not deal with it anymore; as to when we will be through with it; as to when it will be done and finished. But sometimes God says, "Wait! Not yet. Just hold on a little while longer." And that's exactly what we must learn to do.

What does waiting mean? To wait means

- staying in a place or remaining in readiness or in anticipation (until something expected happens);

- remaining or delaying in expectation or anticipation of; awaiting orders or waiting one's turn;[18]

- tarrying.

To realize the value of time, ask someone who has been waiting one hundred years just how much his or her wait time has been worth. Ask how long he or she is willing to wait. Ask how they start their day. How do they end it? Ask how much longer they think they will have to wait. You will probably find that such a person's definition of "wait" is a whole lot different than yours.

When you get to the spot where there is clearly a pause in your life, a minute when time is still and nothing seems to be moving, what do you do? What can you do when in mid-air the feather hangs as if it's going nowhere?

Over one hundred years is a long time to exist in a situation; wouldn't you agree?

Time is for whom?
Asking is for what?

Waiting on God grows you up. It keeps your eyes off yourself and focused on Him. It gives you staying power and praying power. Waiting on God has a way of changing uncertainty into certainty, sadness into joy, crying into moaning, and moaning into rejoicing—even when you are sitting in the valley. It has a way of taking you from all the way down to bringing you all the way up. When one tarries for the Lord in the presence of the Lord, God has a way of showing His goodness. Wait on God.

To all who think they can't take another step, face another day, go through another storm, or endure another valley, wait. To all who ask, "When will this end?" or "How long do I have to endure this?" I say, hold on. Exist. Wait.

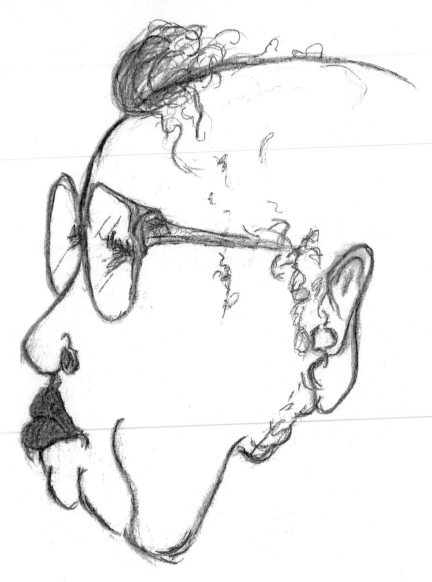

This chapter is dedicated to my grandmother, who
waited over one hundred years to go home.
Bearie Coleman
September 3, 1903—February 1, 2011
Over one hundred years is a long time to exist
in a situation; wouldn't you agree?

CHAPTER 9

PRAISE AND WORSHIP IN THE VALLEY

"Down in my soul cries, Holy.
Down in my soul cries, Holy.
Down in my soul,
in my sanctified soul
Down in my soul
cries, Holy …"[19]

B y the rivers of Babylon, there we sat down, yea, we wept, when we remembered Zion. We hanged our harps upon the willows in the midst thereof. For there they that carried us away captive required of us a song; and they that wasted us required of us mirth, saying, Sing us one of the songs of Zion. How shall we sing the Lord's song in a strange land? – Psalms 137:1-4

This place you are at is strange to you. This is unknown territory — but I implore you to break out. Break out in singing! Break out in praising! Break out!

I've heard that Albert Einstein once used the phrase "as good as dead" to describe people who can no longer wonder and no longer feel amazement. That's how I describe people who can no longer praise God. *I've heard you — and I believe!*

Did you know that we were created to praise God? He manifests His glory and grace and special presence with His people when they offer up true praise and worship to Him. The praises of God's people are the throne upon which He sits; and He inhabits the praises of His people. Do you know what that means? It means He dwells there. He settles there. He tarries there. He remains there to make and to keep house within us. He moves upon this dirt that is the physical body and causes this dirt to sing, to shout, and to raise hands to a holy God.

To fail to worship Him and to give Him praise, on the other hand, is to withhold from God glory that belongs to Him. It is to forget His tender mercies and to be unthankful for His kindness. It is to shut one's eyes to the signs of His presence. To fail to worship Him is to be as good as dead.

"But how can we sing the songs of the LORD while in a pagan land?"

–Psalm 137:4 (NLT)

So far away is home,
but I'm reminded that He's here and near.
He's in my heart, and so
I start to sing a song
so far from home.

"Down in my soul cries, Holy.
Down in my soul cries, Holy..."[20]

I sing and pray all day.
I raise my hands.
I stand and command,
command,
command the praise to come.
I worship Him in a foreign land.
I worship Him.

"Down in my soul cries, Holy.
Down in my soul cries, Holy ..."[21]

There are times in the valley when it's hard to have the zeal, the zest or joy even when I think about what he's done for me. There are times when it's hard to clap my hands or stomp my feet in praise. There are times when the songs and the words mean nothing. *Nothing,* I tell myself. Nothing? I seek for something. And I remind myself of the people mentioned in Psalm 137:1-4: "Alongside Babylon's rivers we sat on the banks; we cried and cried, remembering the good old days in Zion ... Oh, how could we ever sing GOD's song in this wasteland?" (The Message) Just because I'm in the valley does not excuse me from praising Him.

When we consider what He has already done for us, what could be more natural than giving Him praise? What could be more appropriate than to have outbursts of heartfelt praise? Why not lift the hands and lift the voice with an uncontrolled eruption of praise? Why not worship? Why not let His Spirit have His way?

Considering that He is everywhere—even in the valley—why not? Considering His greatness—even in a foreign land—why not? Why shouldn't He be praised? Why not worship Him, even here, even now? Why not rejoice when we still have so much to rejoice about?

To fail to give Him praise is to be as good as dead.

> I rose this morning
> to praise,
> to sing,
> to shout,
> to worship the Lord.

> To know that when I praise
> and when I raise His name,
> He listens.
> He draws near,
> and He listens,
> and He lives within my praise.

How do I beckon the presence of the Lord in a foreign land? I praise, and I raise His name.

How can we sing in the valley? Why should we sing? King Hezekiah declared in Isaiah 38:16-19, "O Lord, by these *things men* live, and in all these *things* is the life of my spirit: so wilt thou recover me, and make me to live…For the grave cannot praise thee, death can *not* celebrate thee…The living, the living, he shall praise thee, as I do this day…" In the end, it all comes down to Him—even when we are in the valley. For that, for Him, I praise!

My weeping turns to joy.
My fear, my sorrow, my doubt turns to hope.
My valley experience turns to praise.

And now, I worship Him
for all He's done, and is doing, and for all He will do.

I take my mind off me,
and all there is of me
             —but He.
I praise.
I worship Him.

"I've got a feeling everything's going to be alright…

Be alright,
Be alright,
Be alright.

My Jesus told me…
Be alright,
Be alright,
Be alright."[22]

CHAPTER 10

COMING OUT

There is another side to everything.
Spring forth, and see what it is to be.

There is a door
that opens way beyond.
It's here; it's near;
just walk.

There is a "yes" that waits
beyond the gates of "maybe so."
You'll never know
if you don't go beyond the gates of "maybe so."
You'll never know.

There is a victory
with a name that sounds like yours.
You'll never know
if you allow yourself to be overshadowed by fear.

How can you hear it clear?
How can you hear?
Have you gotten to the point
where "maybe so" is not enough?
Where "going back" is not an option?
Where "giving up" is way behind you?
Where all you have is "going forward"?
Have you gotten to the point?

There is another side to everything.
Spring forth, and see what it is to be.

"Weeping may endure for a night, but joy cometh in the morning."
-Psalm 30: 5

We wonder when the valley experience is going to end. When will we be through? We all want to get where we're going, but we don't want to have to go through anything to arrive. However, *through* is a process that requires a forward movement or action on one's part. It is not stopping. It is not sitting down and wallowing, and it is definitely not giving up. It is not a permanent position. Instead, it is constantly moving past and beyond. Through assumes that one day what I'm experiencing now will be over. Through assumes there will be joy after weeping; comfort, consolation, and acceptance in the wake of death; peace after the storm; and a mountain after the valley. Through looks forward to tomorrow; it is always seeking and knowing that tomorrow is another day. And God alone knows what tomorrow may bring. Through, then, is looking, and looking, and looking for the face of God until you finally see it. It's never giving up and trusting that you will come out at the appointed time when God decides. Through is a testimony in the making because once you have come through, you have come out.

Through means

- to go in one side and out the other;

- it means to move past limitations or difficulties;[23]

- to move ahead with an expectation of coming out;

- to move beyond where I was;

- that while once in the midst, I am on my way out.

I didn't know what to expect of the valley experience. I didn't know that I would go in one way and come out another. I didn't know that the actions of others would change me. I didn't know that my obedience would grow me. I definitely didn't know that the love of God would keep me. (And, my Lord, I thank You for keeping me!)

Often when a person comes out of a valley experience, he or she will say, "I wouldn't take anything for my journey now." I agree with that statement. I wouldn't take anything for my time in the valley because it was there that I met God. I beheld His glory in so many ways. I felt His presence, and He became as real to me as each and every step I took on my way out.

Yes, there were days when I really wanted to give up. There were days when I could have turned around and gone back. There were days when I sure wanted to sit down and stay put as if to say, "I'm not going any farther, come what may."

The valley experience: it taught me and it brought me to a new level in my life, in my faith, and in my relationship with God.

What's ahead? I have no idea. But I know that grace and mercy—lots of grace and mercy—are behind me. Lives have been touched, stories have been born, faith has been strengthened, tests have been passed, tears have been shed, and prayers have been prayed. Behind me is a valley with my name carved through it, and because of that I bring with me a ray of hope for all who are tired and struggling in their own valley experiences.

Ecclesiastes 7:8 says, "Better is the end of a thing than the beginning thereof." Oh, how I agree with that!

See you on the other side.

"Heavy load, heavy load
God's gonna lighten up my heavy load...
—God's gonna lighten up
my heavy load ...
God's gonna lighten up
My heavy load ..."[24]

I expect to hear a great testimony out of this — I'm waiting and looking for you at the finish line. Love you and always here for you!

(ENDNOTES)

1. Former city manager, John Ware, gave this motto to the city of Dallas.

2. Sandra Crouch, "Completely Yes." <u>Gospel Legacy: Sandra Crouch</u> Light Records, 2008.

3. *Webster's New World Dictionary*, Third College Edition, (Simon and Schuster, 1988) p. 1348. (Definitions have been abbreviated for clarity.)

4. Judson W. Van de Venter and Winfield S. Weeden, "I Surrender All."1855-1939.

5. Priscilla J. Owens, "Jesus Saves." 1882.

6. Ibid.

7. The Clark Sisters, "Is My Living in Vain?" Sony, 1985.

8. *Webster's*, p. 1507.

9. Socrates, *Wisdom Begins in Wonder.*

10. *Matthew Henry Commentary*, Bible Soft. 1992-2001.

11. J.W. Work, "Ride on King Jesus." <u>American Negro Songs</u>, 1940.

12. James Cleveland, "Peace Be Still." Savoy, 1962.

13. Ibid.

14. Ibid.

15. Ibid.

16. Ruth Caye Jones, "In Times Like These." Zondervan Music Publishers, 1944.

17. *Webster's*, p.298.

18. *Webster's*, p.1500.

19. *"Down In My Soul"*, Traditional, The Ingram Gospel Singers. Make My Heart Your Home. Action Music, 1995

20. Ibid.

21. Ibid.

22. O'Landa Draper, *"Gotta Feeling."* Warner Brothers, 1996.

23. *Webster's*, p.1395.

24. The Gospel Imperials, "Heavy Load." Move Satan, 2006.

Sketches

All sketches are by Carmen Beck unless otherwise indicated.

1. Chapter 2, skull and bones illustration by Caleb Beck.

Poetry

All poetry written by Carmen Beck.

CPSIA information can be obtained at www.ICGtesting.com
Printed in the USA
LVOW12s0100190714

395023LV00001B/67/P